BEH●LD
the savior

A 25-DAY CHRISTMAS DEVOTIONAL

BY STEPHEN INGRAM
PUBLISHED BY YM360

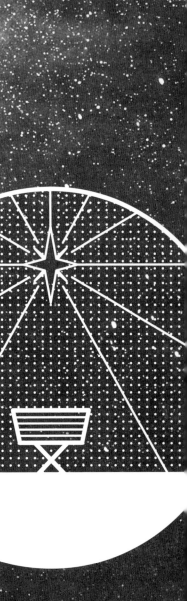

INTRODUCTION

There's nothing like the month leading up to Christmas. Sure, Christmas decorations may go up in October. But when the calendar hits December 1, it gets real. The anticipation begins. Christmas parties. Christmas movies. Christmas break. And then Christmas Eve and Christmas Day.

The anticipation is definitely worth the wait. But there is another kind of Christmas anticipation as well, one that should be at the forefront of our Christmas experience.

Christmas is a time where we prepare our hearts and minds to celebrate the moment that God became human. This anticipation was a feeling that so many in the Christmas story knew well. Mary. Joseph. Elizabeth. Zechariah. The shepherds. The wise men. But have you ever thought that heaven itself was anticipating Jesus' arrival? If you think about it, all of creation was waiting for the moment the long-promised Messiah would burst onto the scene.

Then all at once, He did. He showed up, not with big parades or fanfare on the steps of the Roman emperor's palace. No, the Savior who would take away the sins of the world was born in a humble stable in an off-the-beaten-path town. Born to a teenage mom and a simple but honest dad, the Prince of Peace was suddenly among the very people He created.

And they beheld Him. His parents observed Him in wonder. The shepherds looked down at Him, recalling the angel's message of wonder. The wise men would come to do the same thing. They beheld the Savior. Thousands of years later, we do the same thing.

Christmas is a time for looking once again at the Christ child. The way we do this is by anticipating the celebration of Jesus' birth. That's where these devotions come in. They're designed to help you spend the month of Christmas preparing to celebrate God's gift of His Son.

There's one devotion for each day of the month, except for Christmas Eve and Christmas Day, where there are two for each day (an individual and a family option). We hope you'll find that these 25 days of Christmas devotions get you in the perfect state of mind to truly appreciate the significance of the Savior's arrival.

DAY 1 — What Do You Expect?

"For to us a child is born, to us a son is given; and the government shall be upon his shoulder, and his name shall be called Wonderful Counselor, Mighty God, Everlasting Father, Prince of Peace." - Isaiah 9:6

It's Christmas season! You can feel it in the air. Everywhere you go, you are reminded of that magical day that comes On December 25.

Christmas trees, music on the radio, red bows, twinkling lights, not to mention the excitement that comes along with getting out of school for Christmas break. This is an exciting time of year. Beyond all of the commercials, lights, songs, and shopping, there's something that quietly lies at the heart of this exciting season. It's not found in boxes or even in family gatherings around a festive table. It's the story of a young mother, a reluctant father, and a tiny baby that would change the world forever.

As we enter into this holiday season, I want to challenge you to rethink your holiday and begin to celebrate these *holy* days. In no way am I suggesting that we shouldn't celebrate with presents, singing Jingle Bells, or by drinking hot chocolate. Those are all fun and exciting ways to celebrate this wonderful time of year. Instead, I want you to make sure you're not ONLY expecting presents around a tree or a two-week break from school.

Read Isaiah 9:6 and take a moment to mentally rework what all you're expecting. This verse was a prophecy made hundreds of years before Jesus was born. Through Isaiah, God showed His people what to expect when His Son would one day break through to our world. This expectation is a big part of what Christmas is all about.

If you could make a list of the things you're expecting this Christmas, what would it look like? Where on your list would you find the aspects of our faith that are so important this time of year? Things like hope, joy, peace, and most of all, a Savior?

Starting today, begin looking forward to December 25 by expecting the birth of Jesus. Join me on this journey through the story of His birth as we move from merely celebrating a holiday, to celebrating holy days.

DAY 2 The Angle

"[26] In the sixth month the angel Gabriel was sent from God to a city of Galilee named Nazareth, [27] to a virgin betrothed to a man whose name was Joseph, of the house of David. And the virgin's name was Mary. [28] And he came to her and said, 'Greetings, O favored one, the Lord is with you!'" - Luke 1:26–28

Take a moment and read Luke 1:26-28. Can you even imagine what Mary must have been thinking at this moment? An angel just up and appeared to her. It's not like she got a text from the angel asking if it was OK to drop in. One second there wasn't an angel in her living room, and the next second there was. Talk about a surprise visitor!

Pretty much any time we see an angel in the Bible appearing to someone, there is a familiar message: do not be afraid. Angels were messengers with a word from God for His people. I think it's interesting that so many of their messages started with "do not be afraid." It tells us something about our condition as humans.

We are often fearful. And so the angels often got the "fear not" part out of the way to begin with. However, in the case of the angel that appeared to Mary, it wasn't just a message of "do not be afraid," but a message that told her that things were coming she may not be aware of yet, but that would radically change her life. Mary was about to find herself in a very tough spot, and the angel came to greet her, encourage her, and tell her that she wasn't truly alone. This is why Mary wasn't supposed to be afraid. The radical change that was coming would be a source of God's joy in Mary's life (and for all of creation).

We all have "angels" in our lives, those people who drop into our lives at just the right moment with a message from God. They're not floating beings with halos and wings; they're just people like you and me who God chooses to speak goodness through. Who are your angels? Who have been those people in your life who help you re-center and know that you're not alone? I have had many and hope to have many more. The other piece of this equation to ask is, "who have you been an angel to"?

Some you might know, but I bet there are many people to whom you've been an angel, and you will never find out. I think that's one of the cool parts of how this works. God does things through us without us even knowing sometimes. During this holiday season, pray that God will use you as an angel to speak hope into a life that needs an encouraging word.

DAY 3 Fear Not

"[29] But she was greatly troubled at the saying, and tried to discern what sort of greeting this might be. [30] And the angel said to her, 'Do not be afraid, Mary, for you have found favor with God.'" - Luke 1:29–30

Read Luke 1:29-30. Here we see Mary reacting to the angel's message that she had been chosen as the person to carry God's child. Mary was greatly troubled at his words (understandably so) and wondered what kind of greeting this might be. But the angel said to her, "Do not be afraid, Mary, you have found favor with God."

It may seem unusual to begin such an exciting and festive season with the topic of fear, but remember we're not just thinking about the holidays, but about holy days. This holy season starts with a young teenage girl, engaged and unexpectedly pregnant. Let's be honest: this isn't how most of us would plan on bringing the Savior of humanity into the world. Not anywhere close!

Poor young Mary was scared, and I am sure she felt all alone. It's strange to not only begin the story of Jesus with a pregnant teenager but also in such a scary time and place. So much of the beginning of the story of Jesus' life was a story of fear.

As we enter into this holiday season, fear is one of the things that can begin to creep into our lives. As school begins to wind down, there's a fear of finals and grades coming in. For some of you reading this, there's a fear of time with family over the holidays, as it can be a tough time of year for families who are separated by distance, divorce, or some other factor. Fear of unhealthy family dynamics, fear of not making Christmas "big" or meaningful enough, fear or anxiety about how busy Christmas is, and so on . . . There are aspects of the Christmas season that can cause significant stress on families and can turn these holy days into busy days. It may not be super fun to talk about, but it's a very real part of this season for many people reading this.

As we enter into this holy time of year, I want to challenge you to commit to keeping it holy, less busy, and less fearful. I want to encourage you that while there can be many things to fear this time of year, there are so many more things to look forward to. Work to find the joy in this season. Listen to the angel's words to Mary: "fear not."

DAY 4 — Limitless Possibilities

"And Mary said to the angel, 'How will this be, since I am a virgin?'" - Luke 1:34

You live in a world where logic rules. Where reality wins. There are things you want that you can't have. Some may be relatively fun, like wanting to be a TV star or a famous athlete. Some may be more serious, like wanting your parents to get back together or wanting someone's health to improve. Whatever the case may be, there are plenty of things in life that are simply impossible to have, achieve, or grasp.

And while this is a major bummer, it's just the way it is. Some things just aren't possible.

Except when they are. Except when God gets involved.

Have you ever prayed for something you thought could never happen only to see it happen? Have you ever seen God "open a door" you thought was closed? Have you ever watched God blow away your human-based understanding with a God-sized movement? Mary did.

Mary watched God do the impossible. She watched Him defy the laws of nature. But before she saw the miracle, she doubted the Miracle Maker.

Read Luke 1:34. For a moment, even face-to-face with an angel, Mary had an attack of humanity. "How can this happen?" Mary knew how babies were made, and she knew for a fact she wasn't a candidate! But Mary forgot one thing. The rules that she knew governed the creation of life? The process she was sure she had not been a part of? Mary forgot that God actually set those rules in place. God created the process! Thus, He can work outside the process when He chooses.

It sounds a little oversimplified, but it's true: Nothing is impossible with God. As you prepare your heart to celebrate Jesus' arrival, remember that God is in the business of doing more than we could ever expect. That was true in the Christmas story. And it's true in your life. Spend some time thinking about how this truth impacts your daily life.

DAY 5 It's A Miracle

"[35] And the angel answered her, 'The Holy Spirit will come upon you, and the power of the Most High will overshadow you; therefore the child to be born will be called holy—the Son of God. [36] And behold, your relative Elizabeth in her old age has also conceived a son, and this is the sixth month with her who was called barren. [37] For nothing will be impossible with God.'" - Luke 1:35–37

Miracles are things that we rarely talk about outside of the Bible. While it's a common word in our language, we don't usually speak of them literally but figuratively. "It's a miracle we got to school on time after you took an hour-long shower," or "It's a miracle that our team is still in the playoffs after that loss." We use the word with no real meaning other than something happened that was against the odds. Most civilized people don't believe that if someone touches a blind person's eyes that they'll be healed. That's not something we talk about as modern people, even modern people who believe in God. So what do we do as modern people of faith with the concept of miracles?

First, we have to believe that God has the power to work miracles when and where He chooses simply because He is God. He is the Creator of all things. He has the power to do anything He wills. Second, we have to believe that God still works miracles even though we don't often see them. The world is a big place. How can we know what God is or isn't doing all over the world right now? Third, we may need to reframe what we think of when we think of miracles. I don't automatically think that all miracles are only the sensational kind of miracles we see in Scripture. When I think of a miracle, I think of how God chooses to work in our world in unexpected and beautiful ways. When I see reconciliation between races, it's miraculous. When I see love resurrected from betrayal, it's miraculous. When someone comes out of depression and into health, it's miraculous. It does not have to be flashy to be a miracle.

Read Luke 1:35-37. This is as miraculous a miracle as you could hope to find. God's very Spirit would be the source of the baby in Mary's stomach. And her cousin Elizabeth, who was way past the age where a woman could have a baby, was pregnant as well. These two miracles are at the very heart of the Christmas story.

Where do you see miracles in your life? When have you experienced God in ways where beautiful things are made, and love prevails? Start looking for the miraculous in your world, and I promise you'll find that they're happening all around you. You may have just never noticed.

DAY 6 — Thanks A Lot!

"[46] And Mary said, 'My soul magnifies the Lord, [47] and my spirit rejoices in God my Savior, [48] for he has looked on the humble estate of his servant. For behold, from now on all generations will call me blessed.'" - Luke 1:46–48

Look around you. What in your life brings you joy? This isn't "church answer" time. It's OK to say something like, "my car," or "my family," or even "cheerleading," or "football," or "my guitar." Many things in our lives make us happy. Some of them we think about often (like family or friends). Some of them we may kind of take for granted (like food or our health).

Read Luke 1:46–48. Mary wasn't about to take anything for granted. Again, she had just had a pretty amazing interaction. She had just been told by an angel that she was going to become mi-raculously pregnant with the Son of God. But there was more: her cousin was going to be preg-nant with a baby, too! So, she headed over to see Elizabeth. Now, Elizabeth was super-pumped. Why? She was pregnant with her first child when most women her age had one foot in the grave. (Elizabeth would give birth to John the Baptist.) When Mary and Elizabeth saw each other and shared their news, Mary burst into a meaningful song of thankfulness.

One of the truths about our relationship with God is that He is our provider. He is the giver of good things. He is the source of all your blessings: your health, your life, your shelter, your food, and so on. Sure, God might not literally pay your family's mortgage each month, or put gas in your car. But the money your family earns? The job your mom or dad has? Maybe even the job you have? It's yours through God's grace. All good things come from God.

Mary seemed to have a firm grasp on this. Do you? Are you in the habit of realizing what God has given you and then making sure He hears your thankfulness? It starts with stepping back and seeing that God has given you more than you could ever imagine. When you really under-stand this, praise and thankfulness come naturally.

DAY 7 Shame

"And her husband Joseph, being a just man and unwilling to put her to shame, resolved to divorce her quietly." - Matthew 1:19

Read Matthew 1:19. Can you imagine Mary, a teenage girl, pregnant and alone? Maybe you can. Maybe you have or are experiencing that, or maybe you've been in a place in your life where you felt abandoned, scared, and without hope. I imagine that Mary felt shame; while none of this was her fault, it was still a shameful place to be in. You might know this feeling as well. Maybe your shame is because of something you did, maybe it's because of something that someone else did to you, or maybe it's due to a life situation where no one is at fault, but you still feel ashamed anyways.

There are a couple of things that are important to know about shame. If someone has done something to you that caused you to feel shame, you need to talk to an adult about it. I mean it. Especially if it's something they shouldn't have done, something that has hurt you in some way or another. If it's something that you've done and you feel bad, you need to know that our God is a God that forgives.

God forgives and forgives without question or nuance. Many of us feel shame around this time of year for other reasons, though. We feel shame because we might not have as much money as other families, not get as many presents, deal with separated or dysfunctional families, or that we're dealing with holiday depression.

Each of these things, as well as others, can consume our thoughts and define our actions and moods. When we experience shame, it's important to remember that the mother of our Lord experienced the same thing. But she didn't let it rule her or intimidate her. She listened to God's messenger and found comfort and confidence that she didn't have to be afraid or feel bad. Our God is not a God who delights in shame. Find comfort that God doesn't desire you to feel shame and guilt. These aren't from God.

DAY 8 Choosing Trust

"[24] When Joseph woke from sleep, he did as the angel of the Lord commanded him: he took his wife, [25] but knew her not until she had given birth to a son. And he called his name Jesus." - Matthew 1:24–25

Think of a time when someone told you something you didn't believe. They swore it was true. But for whatever reason, you couldn't bring yourself to believe him or her. Maybe you were on the other end. Have you ever tried to convince someone of something only to be told you weren't telling the truth?

Think about Joseph. Joseph and Mary were to be married, but Mary "was found to be with child." Now, Matthew lets us know that it was the Holy Spirit's work. But, look at Joseph's response: He was going to break off the marriage.

Apparently, Mary told Joseph about the angel, but for whatever reason, Joseph didn't seem willing to believe her. (Or maybe he did, but was unwilling to face the ridicule of his friends and neighbors.) Matthew tells us that Joseph was a good man. But who could have blamed him for wanting out of the marriage? Imagine if your fiancé told you she was pregnant with God's baby. Would you be quick to believe her?

Thankfully, God wasn't done with Joseph. Read Matthew 1:24–25. God sent an angel to tell Joseph that Mary was telling the truth. It must have been bittersweet for Joseph. He must have felt excited to learn what was happening, but maybe a twinge of shame that he didn't stick with Mary in the first place.

The coolest thing about Joseph? His willingness to trust that God would make it all work out. Joseph heard the angel's message and essentially said, "OK. I'm in. I don't understand all this, but I'll trust God."

As Christ-followers, we're called to have the same trust in God. We might not always understand where God is leading us. But like Joseph, we can trust that God is in control. He knows where He's taking us. And that's all that matters.

DAY 9 Pay Attention

"But when the fullness of time had come, God sent forth his Son, born of woman, born under the law." - Galatians 4:4

There is the mall, and then there is the mall at Christmas time. The mall in and of itself can be a pretty overwhelming place, but when it is Christmas, it is a zoo. Everything gets ramped up: the decorations, the number of workers, the displays, and of course, the sales. When you walk through the mall at Christmas, everyone is tugging and pulling at you to try to get your attention and to get you to come into their store and to buy something. It's a constant sensory overload of people wanting things from you. It is a lot like being a teenager nowadays.

When you're in school, there are always things that are competing for your attention: good things, bad things, and things that don't even matter. Each one is pulling and tugging, wanting you to pay attention to what it has to say or asking for what it wants. Friends, enemies, frenemies, teachers, coaches, band directors, dance teachers, grades, clubs, and everything in between, pulls and tugs for your attention and your time. It has to be exhausting.

You live a life today where more is wanted from you than any other generation. You have so many more opportunities and distractions than generations before you, and because of that, you have to learn how to handle them differently than any other generation before you.

Read Galatians 4:4 and think about the concept of time. God's timing is perfect. He knew the exact time to send Jesus into our world. He wasn't a moment too early or a second too late. We don't have God's sense of time. Time for us is fleeting. We're always fighting for more — especially this time of year.

When you go to the mall you can't spend money you do not have; there is only so much you have in your pocket. That money is a lot like your time. Although there are tons of things wanting your attention, you only have so much time that you can give them. There are only so many hours in a day. So budget your time well. Only spend it on things that really matter, and that really make sense in your life. Remember, not everything that wants your attention is something that you need to give your time and attention to.

DAY 10 Good Gifts

"I wish that all were as I myself am. But each has his own gift from God, one of one kind and one of another." - 1 Corinthians 7:7

For some, maybe many, presents or gifts are the main focus of Christmas. I mean, do you blame them? Who doesn't want to receive a gift, out of nowhere, for no reason? You didn't earn it, do anything to deserve it, and may not have even asked for it. It's not only a surprise but a gesture of kindness and love.

For many people, the giving of gifts is equally as enjoyable. We love to see people excited about a gift we've chosen JUST for them. But this Christmas, I want you to think about another kind of gift.

Each of us has gifts that we're called to give. They are a little different than the ones at Christmas. You can't wrap them up and put a bow on them, and you can't find them at a store in the mall. They are gifts that live in you.

Read 1 Corinthians 7:7. God has given every one of us different gifts that are given to be shared with the world. Think about it: What are you good at? What are the things you really have a passion for and do well? What are the things that live in you that you know or are discovering that you can give to the world? These don't have to be things that we usually label as being "spiritual." When we do this, we're limiting God. We usually think of these gifts as things like praying, interpreting the Bible, telling others about Jesus, and so on. And these are definitely gifts from God. But there are other gifts, too. Being really good at math, being an excellent artist, or having a knack for working with animals are all gifts God has given you.

Whatever God has gifted you with, live into it, and know that all gifts that you have can be given to others and the world in God's name.

Christmas is a time for gifts. Now go and give your gift to the world.

DAY  Journey Together

"And Joseph also went up from Galilee, from the town of Nazareth, to Judea, to the city of David, which is called Bethlehem, because he was of the house and lineage of David." - Luke 2:4

Several years ago, I was in Israel for a pilgrimage. "Pilgrimage" is just a fancy word for a trip where you go to holy places and seek to know God more through those experiences. While I was in Israel, I had the privilege of going on a journey from Nazareth to the town of Bethlehem. This is the same journey that Mary and Joseph took so many years ago. Well sort of.

Read Luke 2:4. Can you imagine what their journey was like? I can. You see, when I took the journey, I didn't ride a mule or a camel. I rode in a car. I had air conditioning, which is a good thing, too, because it got up to 115 degrees that day. We were able to stop and get supplies as we needed, and we were never worried about bandits on the road robbing us. I didn't have to worry about finding somewhere to stay the night.

Come to think about it, I don't remember worrying about anything on my journey that day. It was relatively uneventful, other than the important parts like visiting the sites, which was amazing. I imagine Mary and Joseph's journey being so much more difficult than mine and full of uncertainty. That's the way life is sometimes; you don't know what the journey will hold. Sometimes it will be full of excitement and promise — other times, full of fear and uncertainty.

No matter where you are in your journey and what type of journey you're on, I want to encourage you that God is with you on that journey. God was with Mary and Joseph, and God will be with you.

That doesn't mean the journey will be any easier or go as planned. It just means that no matter what happens, you will never journey alone.

DAY 12 Timely Detour

" . . . to be registered with Mary, his betrothed, who was with child." - Luke 2:5

A lot of times, when we think about Bethlehem, we think of children's plays and Christmas cards with a perfectly clear night sky and a picturesque wooden stable. That's a comforting image to us. But the truth is that Bethlehem was not supposed to happen for Mary and Joseph. For all we know, they didn't have many friends in Bethlehem. Bethlehem was foreign. Bethlehem was a detour; it wasn't the destination. Bethlehem wasn't inviting. It proved to be inhospitable. Bethlehem was an accident. It definitely wasn't home.

They weren't planning on being there. They had somewhere else they had to be. They had other plans. Then Jesus came. When Jesus came, it put Mary and Joseph in a spot they hadn't intended to be in.

They had to improvise and do it quickly.

Read Luke 2:5. The first Christmas may very well have been nothing like we imagine it to be. I bet a lot of your Christmases are similar in that way. It just doesn't look like the television shows and Christmas cards portray it. It's messy, rarely goes as planned, and can be pretty tough to deal with sometimes. Just like the first Christmas, we set up expectations as to what Christmas is "supposed" to look like. Sometimes, it goes as planned. Other times, we find ourselves feeling disappointed because we subscribe to expectations that are not based on realities but on ideals.

Bethlehem was tough, and it was messy. But look what came out of it. Just because your family is a little messed up or things do not go exactly as planned does not mean that Christmas isn't just as meaningful. It can be and should be. This Christmas, lets lower the expectations based on movies and cards, and let's set it in grace, peace, and hope for imperfect people and families.

DAY  Hope

"And while they were there, the time came for her to give birth." - Luke 2:6

Hope is a word that's used a lot around Christmas.

"I hope your brother will be able to come home from college this Christmas."
"I hope this year will be less busy than the last"
"I hope I get everything I asked for from Santa!"

Read Luke 2:6. Christmas is a season of hope. It's a time where we celebrate the coming of Christ into the world. Through the darkest of situations, in one of the most difficult of times, God brought this light into the world. We know that hope exists because Christ was born.

I do wonder, with how often and in how so many ways the word is used, what hope really means to us today? I think that if we think about it and the way we use it, it doesn't reflect the kind of hope that God calls us to. Usually, when we talk about hope, it's something we're not certain will happen or that we want to happen. When we see hope in the Bible, as people of faith, we get to hope differently. We get to hope, believing that God already has given us a promise.

We don't hope aimlessly, simply wanting something. We hope believing that something is already in the works and that God is already up to something. We hope, not in spite of what might happen, but believing that something better is already happening as we speak.

What do you hope for this Christmas? Do you trust that God will meet your needs in a way that is best for you?

DAY 14 Away in a Manger

"And she gave birth to her firstborn son and wrapped him in swaddling cloths and laid him in a manger, because there was no place for them in the inn." - Luke 2:7

Read Luke 2:7. Sometimes our expectations for our lives don't match up with God's expectations for our lives. If I'm honest, I would have never chosen to bring the Savior of the World into the world the way God chose to. Here's how I would have gone about it:

First, I would've had Jesus born into a family that mattered, someone with influence. If nothing else, I would've had Him born to someone that was at least married! Also, let's not have a census that's going to drag them away from friends and family. Let's have them set up at home, nice and happy so that others can be there to be a part of this monumental event.

This leads me to my next point: No Publicity. What? OK, sure, a star. But there are lots of stars. Why not a giant arrow in the sky with big flashy letters saying "Jesus"? Also, Bethlehem? Why couldn't God have waited until they were a little further down the road in Jerusalem? Jerusalem ... that's a big place full of important people, not Bethlehem.

Then we have the shepherds and wise men. Not exactly the press or dignitaries I would've brought to the table. (Well, at least the wise men brought some good gifts.) Finally, the stable and manger. Nope. Not happening. If I couldn't find a giant mansion, I'd at least have Jesus born somewhere He didn't have to compete with cows for sleeping quarters.

I say all of this jokingly to make a point: the Son of God, the one who would change everything, broke out of heaven and into this earth to a hay-trough borrowed from feeding animals. A manger ... Bethlehem ...

My way makes way more sense to me. But that's why God's ways are different and better than mine. They are better and different from yours, too. And that's a good thing for both of us. Celebrate this truth today.

DAY 15 The Shepherds, Part 1

"[8] And in the same region there were shepherds out in the field, keeping watch over their flock by night. [9] And an angel of the Lord appeared to them, and the glory of the Lord shone around them, and they were filled with great fear. [10] And the angel said to them, 'Fear not, for behold, I bring you good news of great joy that will be for all the people. [11] For unto you is born this day in the city of David a Savior, who is Christ the Lord. [12] And this will be a sign for you: you will find a baby wrapped in swaddling cloths and lying in a manger.'" - Luke 2:8–12

Read Luke 2:8-12. Check out what is happening in this amazing encounter. The Bible says that there were shepherds who were looking after their sheep that night. They were approached by angels and told about Jesus. Can you imagine what it must have been like to be minding your own business and then suddenly angels appeared, lighting up the sky with their glory? These shepherds listened to the angels. They left their fields, and they saw what God had promised them. Then, after seeing Jesus, they began to spread the word about what they'd seen.

It didn't say that they saw Jesus, memorized a lot of facts about Him, decided a good strategy to talk about what they knew, and then went and spread the word. It just says that they went.

I love the shepherds' enthusiasm. If you noticed, it doesn't say that they went and tried to convince people to come and worship this baby, nor does it say that they had it all figured out before they went. It just says that they went and told what they had experienced and what had been told to them about this baby.

First, I want you to think about what you've experienced with God. How has God made Himself known to you? How has He changed you? Secondly, what have others told you about their experience with God? Lastly, who was the last person you told about your experience? I don't mean who's the last person you invited to church. Inviting people to church is not a bad thing. It's a good thing. But Jesus never tells us that the sum of the sharing of our faith should be an invitation for someone to join us at church. Jesus DOES tell us repeatedly that we should tell the truth about who He is and about our experiences with Him. There's a difference.

The shepherds wanted others to know what they had experienced. What have you experienced? How can that be helpful to others? What will you tell them about Jesus?

"And an angel of the Lord appeared to them, and the glory of the Lord shone around them, and they were filled with great fear." - Luke 2:9

Have you ever been in a situation where suddenly your assumptions or thoughts about a specific person or thing were pretty much blown off the map? Maybe it was the moment you realized the little test you were "prepared" for was really an overwhelming obstacle you had no chance of conquering. Or the moment you realized that he or she really does like you a lot! Or how about the moment you realized your team is completely overmatched. Or . . . Well, you get the point. There are moments of clarity where what you thought was the case may not necessarily be the case at all.

The shepherds who were in the fields outside of Bethlehem? They experienced one of those moments in a big, big way.

Read Luke 2:9. It's safe to say that the shepherds knew God. Or they knew of Him as well as they could. They were Israelites. They were, after all, God's people. But, everything they thought they knew about God and His ways were pretty much overwhelmed that night. All of a sudden, the God who was a little distant and a lot mysterious was right up in their world. In their faces!

Look at the description in verse 9: "the glory of the Lord shone around them." Can you imagine? God was no longer an idea; He was real. He had broken the invisible barrier between His Kingdom and this world. And it's entirely safe to say the world was never the same. Isn't that a pretty good way to think about the Christmas story in general? Isn't it really as simple as God breaking the barrier and coming into our world? It is that simple. Yet, the power behind this simple truth is life-changing.

You are who you are today because God chose to send His Son into this world. Let that truth sink in and impact the way you live your life today.

DAY 17 The Shepherds, Part 3

"And they went with haste and found Mary and Joseph, and the baby lying in a manger." - Luke 2:16

We know it all. We've seen it all. It's tough to slip something past us that we haven't heard of before. While this isn't exactly true, we've been conditioned to feel like it is. With the prevalence of information at our fingertips, it certainly feels like just about everything worth knowing is available to be known.

And when we do see something we haven't seen before, we tend not to believe it's real. When every celebrity is Photoshopped to perfection, when every movie is CGI'd to the point where we don't know what's real and what isn't. . . who can blame us?

You might say we've lost our sense of wonder. And that's a bad thing. Wonder is like curiosity times ten. It's the spirit of discovery. It's looking at the world around us with a healthy dose of "I can still be impressed, surprised, and amazed."

Read Luke 2:16. The shepherds had a huge sense of wonder. They had just been witness to a holy concert, a heavenly performance unlike any ever heard. And they were amazed. They were like, "Wow!" (Or something like that.) Moved by this, they took off running, acting on their strong sense of wonder, heading out to discover if what they had been told was true.

And of course, they found that it was true. As true as anything could ever be. Their wonder was rewarded. They were amazed. Moved. Transfixed. All because they possessed an amazing curiosity and openness about God and His ways.

How is your sense of wonder?

DAY 18 The Wise Men, Part 1

"[7] Then Herod summoned the wise men secretly and ascertained from them what time the star had appeared. [8] And he sent them to Bethlehem, saying, 'Go and search diligently for the child, and when you have found him, bring me word, that I too may come and worship him.'" - Matthew 2:7–8

Read Matthew 2:7–8. The Gospel of Matthew tells us about a group of wise men who came to visit Jesus, worship Him, and give Him gifts. Sometimes these men are referred to as kings, but most scholars believe that they were priests of another religion who came to Jesus because they focused on and read the stars. There's something about Christmas that attracts all sorts of people, not just people who call themselves Christians.

At Christmas, especially in the US, it doesn't matter if you have not been to church in the whole year, you will probably find yourself at some sort church around Christmas. Something about the season attracts all sorts of people, not just those who actively follow Christ.

Just like the Magi, they come. My question is, "what will they find when they come"? Sometimes we do everything we can to attract people to Christianity, and when they finally come, we don't have a lot to show them. We must have a faith that is authentic and real, or else we run the risk of bringing them to a stable with an empty manger.

Who are the Magi in your life? Who are those people who are interested in the faith but are not yet convinced? I bet you have friends like that at school and on your teams. Or maybe at your job. I would also bet that there are even a number of people in your youth group who aren't quite convinced yet either.

So what kind of faith will you show them? Is it a faith that's deeply meaningful, thoughtful, and full of passion? Or will it be a faith that disappoints when they get too close? They are seeking. What will be there when they arrive?

DAY 19 Following The Star

"When they saw the star, they rejoiced exceedingly with great joy." - Matthew 2:10

A star. There are millions of them in the sky. I remember one night down in Central America, in Panama. There were no artificial lights for miles and miles, and the night was crystal clear. I was blown away by the incredible number of stars I could see that night. I've never seen anything like it. But for some reason, this one star stood out from all of the others that night. It made me think of the star in the Christmas story.

Read Matthew 2:10. There was something about that one star, guiding others to the place where Jesus was born. I often wonder what it looked like. Was it a different shape? Was it brighter than the rest? Something was different. Something made it stand out amid millions of others. The truth is that the star stood out because it had a purpose. Its purpose was to be different. And it was different enough to grab other's attention and direct them to Bethlehem.

There are over 6 billion people in our world. Sometimes I feel like just one among those billions. I bet you do too. The difference is that we have a reason to stand out. We have a reason to shine brighter and be bolder than so many of the others. Jesus told us to be salt and light. We're called to stand out to be different and to show others, through the night, where Jesus is.

So many times, there are people who shine bright and only bring attention to themselves. We have the opportunity to shine and stand out and then point others to God. For some, the world can be a dark, cold place. What will you do to shine bright and show the way to Jesus?

"And going into the house, they saw the child with Mary his mother, and they fell down and worshiped him. Then, opening their treasures, they offered him gifts, gold and frankincense and myrrh." - Matthew 2:11

Read Matthew 2:11. I think that it's such a cool part of the story that the wise men brought gifts to this baby. I picture them laying these really expensive gifts of gold, frankincense, and myrrh around His little manger. Interestingly, those gifts are not really for a baby; they're for other times in a person's life. I bet they didn't know what Jesus would do with them, but they brought them anyway. We're called to do the same thing.

We're called to bring our gifts to Jesus, no matter what they are or what we think Jesus will do with them. Our call is to bring them and commit them to God. Sometimes, in churches, we make the mistake of valuing certain gifts over others. In churches, we often over-value gifts like leadership, singing, and speaking, to name a few, and this is wrong. Just because you don't do the "up front" stuff doesn't mean that God can't do just as much (if not more) with your gifts. A lot of times, because we value some over others, it keeps away people with less up-front gifts.

I don't care if you are an incredible writer, or you can fix a car, or you can kick a soccer ball the length of the field, God wants you to bring those gifts and offer them. No matter what you do, you need to remember that you have the option to do it for God.

This doesn't mean that every time you write a fantastic poem that you need to kneel and do a prayer before you submit it to the teacher. It just means that when you do these things, you understand them as an act of worship. It also means that through your gifts, you try to make the world a better place for people everywhere.

DAY 21 A "Normal" Family

"And if it is evil in your eyes to serve the LORD, choose this day whom you will serve, whether the gods your fathers served in the region beyond the River, or the gods of the Amorites in whose land you dwell. But as for me and my house, we will serve the LORD." - Joshua 24:15

So, I bet that most of you wouldn't say that your family is completely normal. Right? I mean, let's face it, we're all just a little (if not a lot) weird. We all have our quirks, strange habits, and imperfections that keep us from being the Brady Bunch. Few times is this more evident than at Christmas time. The stress, tension, and hectic pace of Christmas bring out some very interesting moments in a family.

Here's the good news: there's no such thing as normal, especially when it comes to families. Now, don't get me wrong: some families make it look "normal," but when it comes down to it, we all have our problems. So did Jesus and His family.

Think about it. Mary was probably a teenager. There was some pretty serious scandal around the pregnancy. Joseph was seeing angels. They had the baby while on a really rough journey and ended up, according to at least one biblical account, fleeing to Egypt. Yep, they had some issues. Joseph is not even mentioned after the birth of Jesus, whereas Mary is throughout the life of Jesus. It couldn't have been easy. They also had a blended family. We know that Jesus had siblings, and we also know that Joseph was not Jesus' biological dad.

See? It wasn't perfect by any means. But it worked.

Read Joshua 24:15. What about your family? What makes you different? Blended? Divorced? Still together but a little crazy? A brother or sister who is a little wild? During this holiday season, make sure not to let that get you down. All of our families are a little crazy, even Jesus' family. When you think about it, that's what normal family looks like. Enjoy your normal family this Christmas!

"Your kingdom is an everlasting kingdom, and your dominion endures through-out all generations. [The LORD is faithful in all his words and kind in all his works.]" - Psalm 145:13

Read Psalm 145:13. So the first thing about a Christmas tree is that it is totally not in the Bible. I mean, it would've been cool if the shepherds would've brought a little shrub from the desert and had the wise men decorated it with gems. That would be cool if that were how we got our Christmas tree tradition. But it's not.

There are several origin stories for the Christmas tree, but the most probable is that they orig-inated in Germany in the 1500s. So why does it matter? Well, for me, it matters because it's a place where we gather. If your home is like mine, my wife, my three kids, and I go and pick out a tree together, which is a big deal, of course. We then take it in, untie it, put it in the holder, and together we decorate it.

Our Christmas tree doesn't have a lot of fancy decorations that we bought at a store. It's covered by hand made decorations and decorations that were ours when we were kids and have been passed down. As we take each decoration out of the box, there is a story that comes with each. My first Christmas. My wife's ornament from when she was born. One that my great grand-mother, who died when I was a baby, gave me (it is my favorite). And so on.

Our kids have special ornaments too. They have ornaments that they made, and some that have their pictures from when they were babies. We hang them, decorate the tree, and then finally light the entire thing.

Why is a tree important? Because it is a place to share stories, old memories, and make new memories with family that will be shared for lifetimes. It doesn't have to be a tree, but it's so important to share stories as family and friends. What are your traditions that bring you closer to your family?

DAY 23 Stockings

"Give thanks to the LORD, for he is good, for his steadfast love endures forever."
- Psalm 136:1

Read Psalm 136:1. Again, stockings are definitely not in the Bible. But that's OK! Not all traditions have to be. The original story behind hanging stockings was that the socks, also known as stockings, were hung by the fireplace to dry out after being soaked from walking around outside in the snow. Then when Santa Clause came, these stockings were filled with fruit and nuts, and if someone were really lucky, a small toy. There were no stacks of presents around a tree. There were no boxes on top of boxes of lavish gifts. It was only some fruit, nuts, and maybe a trinket of sorts.

When I look at our stockings, I can't help but be reminded that no matter what we "get" for Christmas, we should be so thankful. Sometimes people get wrapped up in trying to get the perfect presents or making sure that a certain dollar amount is spent. Some people even will become depressed or upset when they don't get what they want. Stockings remind me that most of us already have everything we need anyways. It's incredible just how much we all have, and how much we don't need.

This is not a devotion to make you feel bad about what you have, but to help you feel grateful and content with what you don't have. So as you hang your stockings by the chimney with care, make sure you also hang them with gratitude and thanksgiving for all we have.

DAY 24 Christmas Eve

"[1] In those days a decree went out from Caesar Augustus that all the world should be registered. [2] This was the first registration when Quirinius was governor of Syria. [3] And all went to be registered, each to his own town. [4] And Joseph also went up from Galilee, from the town of Nazareth, to Judea, to the city of David, which is called Bethlehem, because he was of the house and lineage of David, [5] to be registered with Mary, his betrothed, who was with child." - Luke 2:1–5

You may have a younger brother or sister whom you can remember being born. You might remember some excitement and some anxiety as your parents waited for this new baby to come into the world. As a parent of three kids, I can't describe to you how incredible and how nerve-wracking it is leading up to your child being born. In a day with modern medicine, technology, cars, and hospitals, we have it pretty easy when it comes to having babies.

Read Luke 2:1–5. In the days of Mary and Joseph, it wasn't anywhere near as pleasant. It was also not too pleasant that they were on the road, away from home, with nowhere to stay. It had to be completely crazy for this man and especially his young bride. I couldn't imagine just how anxious they were as they waited on God to send His only son into the world through Mary.

Sometimes we find ourselves waiting on God to come into our situations. We wait nervously, trusting that God has a plan and will do what He needs to do. But it can be so nerve-wracking, full of fear, and anxiety. As people of faith, we have faith in God that He will not leave us out to dry. But sometimes waiting drives us crazy. When I'm in these situations, I can't help but think of Mary and Joseph on that night so long ago. Waiting. Waiting and waiting some more. They just had to wait for what God was going to do.

Amid a very scary time in history, and a very scary part of the world, all they could do was wait on the miracle that God was going to perform in their lives. On this Christmas eve, I encourage you, even as you wait for the amazingly fun day that tomorrow will bring, think about how Mary and Joseph and how they waited on the work that God would do in their world.

DAY 24 Christmas Eve (Family)

"[1] In those days a decree went out from Caesar Augustus that all the world should be registered. [2] This was the first registration when Quirinius was governor of Syria. [3] And all went to be registered, each to his own town." - Luke 2:1–3

On this Christmas Eve, ask if your family can sit together and read the Christmas story together.

Most know the version that is in Luke 2:1- 21. Read this together, maybe even different members of the family reading different parts.

When you finish, ask what everyone's favorite part was and why.

Then go and do something fun together, make some hot chocolate, or wassail. Watch a Christmas movie, or play a board game.

Whatever you do, make sure to do it together.

DAY 25 Christmas Day

"[6] And while they were there, the time came for her to give birth. [7] And she gave birth to her firstborn son and wrapped him in swaddling cloths and laid him in a manger, because there was no place for them in the inn." - Luke 2:6–7

Read Luke 2:6-21. Focus on verses 6-7. It's a beautiful day. Today is one of the two most holy days of the Christian year. Today is a day to celebrate, be with friends and family, and remember the day that our Lord was born into this world.

I will not write a long devotion today because there are a lot of things you should be doing other than reading my words. But I will challenge you with this: Read the nativity story. Take your time and read it slowly. Don't rush but read each word taking it in and imagining the story playing out in front of you. Be grateful for what happened and know that God still births miracles in our world today.

Even in the most uncertain of places, God is still doing amazing work. Read the story again. Go and be with the people you love and the people who love you. Celebrate, laugh, smile, take a nap, and know that our God loves us so much that He sent His son into this pretty crazy world to live, to love, and to show us a better way.

Go and live that better way today.

DAY 25 Christmas Day (Family)

"[13] And suddenly there was with the angel a multitude of the heavenly host praising God and saying, [14] 'Glory to God in the highest, and on earth peace among those with whom he is pleased!'" - Luke 2:13–14

It's Christmas morning. There's so much anticipation and excitement. Your parents are probably pretty tired, so if you can, help them out and be patient. Before you all open your presents, take a moment together, and each person answer this one question about each person in the room:

I'm thankful to God for you because _____ .

This is a great way to start your day in a way that's not focused around presents, but the gift that God has given you as a family. The gifts that truly matter.

Merry Christmas!!!!

ABOUT THE AUTHOR

Stephen is a dad, husband, writer, and foodie. He has served in churches since 1998 and also has served as a lead consultant with Ministry Architects since 2009. He lives in Homewood, AL, with his wife, Mary Liz, and their three kids Mary Clare, Patrick, and Nora Grace. Stephen has his undergraduate from Samford University, where he majored in Religion and his Masters of Divinity from McAfee School of Theology. Stephen speaks at conferences all around the country, as well as leading training events, spiritual parenting workshops, and retreats for youth ministries. He is currently the Pastor of Students and Missions at Grace, A United Methodist Congregation. His books include Hollow Faith: How Andy Griffith, Facebook, and the American Dream Neutered the Gospel, ExtraOrdinary Time: 365 Ordinary Moments with an Anything But Ordinary God; and Organic Student Ministry. Stephen deeply loves working with students and their families, growing, nurturing, and challenging their faith as they strive to answer the questions: Who am I and Why am I here?

YOU KNOW IT'S IMPORTANT TO GROW CLOSER TO GOD

YM360 DEVOTIONALS CAN HELP

Student devotionals from YM360 help you stay close to God by equipping you to creatively and relevantly dig-in to His Word.